THE WORLD'S SAILING

SHIPS

© EDIMAT BOOKS Ltd. London
is an affiliate of Edimat Libros S.A.
C/ Primavera, 35 Pol. Ind. El Malvar
Arganda del Rey - 28500 (Madrid) Spain
E-mail: edimat@edimat.es

Title: *The World's Sailing Ships*
Author: *Camil Busquets i Vilanova*

ISBN: 84-9794-000-8
Legal Deposit: M-48231-2004

PRINTED IN SPAIN

THE WORLD´S SAILING SHIPS

Camil Busquets i Vilanova

Prologue

THE MAJESTY OF SAILING SHIPS

It is now many years since the serene and elegant beauty of sailing ships disappeared from the ocean waves. These days our only remaining testimony to their splendour is the few surviving vessels from the old days of grandeur, moored alongside the newer designs. Also beautiful, it cannot be denied, but despite their efforts they simply lack the elegance and majesty of the *Windjammers* and *Clippers* of yesteryear.

There is more evidence of the age of the sailing ship in the reconstruction of historic ships, which for various reasons were historically of interest to a country, group, organisation, association or training school, and have been restored to new glory. Within this category we can also include ships that have been recovered by museums or private owners, many of which fly the flag and bear the name of an institution, city or country.

Besides these reconstructed vessels, untiring fighters in the titanic struggle against the disappearance of the traditional sailing ship in the wake of the machine, are each and every one of the leisure yachts preserved by their owners with great effort and love. These are the classic yachts which participate in most of the meetings, regattas rather than competitions, reserved exclusively for ships of a certain age and status, which even when their appearance is somewhat diminished still deserve the classification of "great sailing ships", as the description refers not to the size of the ship but to her presence. That is because, as anybody who has ever sailed on board a classic yacht will know, every one of them has a soul.

Other great ships exist that have been preserved for a variety of reasons, perhaps thanks to the specific wishes of an unknown person or due to the simple coincidence of being in the right place at the right time. In the same way, there are so many ships that have been lost to us, for the opposite reason that their days happened to end at an unfortunate time, place or occasion.

To all of them, those of the past and those of the present, and to those people who make it possible for us to still enjoy the ones we do have, we dedicate our thanks, our respect and our most profound admiration.

CHAPTER I

Square rig ships

The four-mast ship Kruzenshtern *was formerly the Windjammer* Padua, *belonging to the famous German company Flying P and built, in 1926, in the German shipyards of Tecklenborg in Bremerhaven. At the end of the Second World War she passed into Russian hands.*

Square rigging is the commonest kind in large ships and has been a constant feature of ocean vessels. Although the sails are square their shape forms a semi-circle with the mast as the diameter and the circumference points at either end of the yardarm. This type of rigging makes the form of a cross, as the yard is horizontal to the mast.

Square sails date back many years, and their use goes back as far as the earliest history of sailing, to Assyrian, Phoenician, Carthaginian, Romans and Viking ships, though these models did not reach the perfection achieved in the period between the discovery of America in 1492 and the French Revolution in 1789.

Square rigging was considered ideal for ocean voyages, as it was the best way of utilising a constant and regular wind. This is more or less what was needed for the carracks, caravels and galleons that took advantage of the winds on their voyages from Europe to America, and from America to Asia or Africa, and for this reason these winds are called the *trade-winds*, as the important ocean voyages of commerce of the sixteenth, seventeenth, eighteenth and nineteenth centuries depended on their strength.

In fact Christopher Columbus, a wise sailor, changed part of the rigging of his caravels *Pinta* and *Niña* from lateen sails to square ones, to assure a good voyage across the Atlantic. Of course, a ship can never be totally square rigged; her design makes her inferior to the gaff-rig for sailing close to the wind (sailing at a greater or lesser angle against the wind), and therefore the usual way is for square rigged ships to use other triangular lateen sails when they want to sail close to the wind.

THE DEVELOPMENT OF SQUARE RIGGING

Mythology attributes the invention of the sail to the Egyptian goddess Isis, and more specifically, the square sail, as on one occasion she is said to have held her cloak with both hands and let the wind fill it to propel the ship she was aboard. This is a very poetic story, but probably untrue.

It is very difficult to investigate when and where the first square sail in history appeared. However, what does seem to be fact is the existence of square sails on the Egyptian ships that

Nomenclature of the sails of a Clipper *from the nineteenth century (according to Redereij Clipper Stad Amsterdam / Phil Evans, Paasch, Underhill and others)*

01 *Flying jib*
02 *Jib*
03 *Inner jib*
04 *Fore topmast staysail*
05 *Foresail*
06 *Lower fore topsail*
07 *Upper fore topsail*
08 *Topgallant foresail*
09 *Royal*
10 *Topmast staysail*
11 *Main topgallant staysail*
12 *Main royal staysail*
13 *Mainsail*
14 *Lower topsail*
15 *Upper topsail*
16 *Main topgallant sail*
17 *Main royal*
18 *Main skysail*
19 *Mizzen topmast staysail*
20 *Mizzen staysail*
21 *Mizzen sail*
22 *Mizzen topmast sail*
23 *Mizzen topgallant sail*
24 *Mizzen royal*
25 *Spanker sail*
26 *Fore topmast studding sail*
27 *Fore topgallant studding sail*

When a sail is unfolded into two parts they are usually differentiated into upper and lower, and if more sails are attached on top of the royal sails they are called "skysail" plus the rest of the name, which results in terms such as "Mizzen skysail". Generally, the skysails were fastened to a royal mast, but other examples of rigging also exist. In extreme cases, another sail called the moonsail was hoisted on top of the skysail. And in the sixteenth century, the rectangular bonnet sail could be added to the lower part of the mainsail to make the most of light winds.

The barque Europa *coming into port at Cádiz in the south of Spain to take part in the Cádiz 2000 Regatta. This ship was built in Hamburg, in 1911, as a boat lighthouse for the mouth of the River Elbe, and stayed in service until the early seventies.*

The barque Europe, *which we can here see under full sail – except the lower studding sails, was built in the Stülcken shipyards in Hamburg and called* Senator Brockes.

The Kruzenshtern *is one of the most easily recognisable tall ships due to her being painted in black and white bands in the style of the old Clippers. Her sails have a total surface area of 38,244 square feet and her regular crew was made up of 220 students of the Russian Ministry of Fishing.*

round about 3500 BC were making commercial voyages around the west coast of Africa and as far as the Mozambique Channel. These vessels had a single sail supported by a bipod mast, which could be folded down on deck with relative ease, as these used a combination of sails and oars, making the mast on some occasions more of a hindrance than anything else.

Twenty centuries later, towards the year 1500 BC, in Egypt as well, we also hear about larger vessels with similar rigging and conditions appropriate for seafaring. But it was the circumnavi-

FOLLOWING PAGE: *The barque* Gorch Fock *is a Bundesmarine training ship. Here, we can see her arrival in Cádiz to participate in the Cádiz 2000 Regatta. The German navy called its training ship* Gorch Fock *after the First World War as this was the pen name of the writer Johannes Kinau, who died on board the* Wiesbaden *in the Battle of Jutland.*

The modern tall ships usually have a mixed rig, which can be fairly unorthodox. Such is the case of this brig-schooner Sui Generis, *which in addition to being fitted out with one-piece masts, uses a profusion of different types of sails (Photo: Javier Sánchez García).*

HMS Lord Nelson, *which we can here see pictured against the Magdalena Palace, Santander, Spain, is even more famous, if possible, because its design allows for the embarkation of partially handicapped students (Photo: Javier Sánchez García).*

The Russian four-mast ship Sedov, *formerly the German* Margaret Vinnen, *is one of the largest tall ships still sailing today. This one works as a training ship, and occasionally operates chartered voyages (Photo: Javier Sánchez García).*

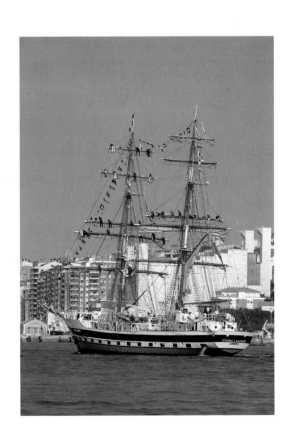

The Stavros S. Niarchos *is a square-rig brig and training ship belonging to the Sail Training Association, although this classification could be questioned according to the canons of the most traditional naval architecture (Photo: Javier Sánchez García).*

Another view of the Goch Fock. Also 'plying the waves', under full sail, about to set out in the Cádiz-2000 Regatta.

An interesting characteristic of the vast majority of the German barques is that their spanker sail is divided into two parts, upper and lower, which dates back to the beginning of the twentieth century. View of the Goch Fock from her port quarter showing her double spanker sail and gaff topsail.

gation of the African continent by ships of Pharaoh Necao II in 616 BC when the square rig must have been noticeably improved, because such a voyage depends on many different types of runs relative to the prevailing wind.

The Phoenicians, Assyrians and Greeks also exclusively used the square sail, although at times they would use two, one extra at the bow, which on Roman ships was known as an *artimon*, a term originating from Greek which came to mean something similar to the mizzen sail.

For a long time, Mediterranean sailing used mixed propulsion by means of oars in addition to one or two square rigs, although at some point lateen sails came to be more predominant.

FOLLOWING PAGE: *The Venezuelan training barque* Simón Bolívar *during the parade prior to the Cutty Sark '96, sailing with auxiliary engine and with her sails set. Note that strangely enough the gaff topsail is raised but not the spanker, which is unusual with a rather complicated manoeuvring sail.*

The British Jubilee Sailing Trust barque
Lord Nelson. *This ship was specially built*
to operate with handicapped students, so
that her rigging can be raised and lowered
automatically.

The Eye of the Wind *using her engine. Built in*
1911 as the Friedrich *at the Konrad Luhring*
shipyards in Germany, she is a schooner with
topsail rigging.

Entering into the Middle Ages – from the fall of the Roman Empire in the fifth century AD to the taking of Constantinople (1453) and/or the discovery of America (1492) – Atlantic vessels began to be built by the Normans, the so-called "men of the north", incorporating several developments.

The Vikings or Normans always used just one large sail in their speedy, lightweight – and also feared – vessels, and this sail can be considered the first to sail Atlantic waters, since we should recall that the reconstructions of the balsa rafts with which the Norwegian anthropologist Thor Heyerdahl set out to prove his theory used precisely this type of sail. The *Ra* and *Ra II* attempted to demonstrate that Mediterranean peoples could have reached American shores as early as in the time of the Egyptians.

The barque Lord Nelson *at full sail. The boom has an upper passageway to assist disabled sailors, since one of her main purposes is to offer naval training to the physically handicapped.*

In the slow evolution of the vessels of those times, an evolution that led to vessels such as carracks, cogs, naos, hookers and others, the most common ships had three masts – the foremast, the mainmast and the mizzenmast – with the fore and mainmasts fitted out with square rigging and the mizzenmast with lateen sails, i.e., the exvoto rigging called the Coca of Mataró or the Catalan Nao, known worldwide. A spritsail at the bow, under the bowsprit, and a small topsail over the mainsail, were also added. Such is the rigging of the *Santa María*, Christopher Columbus' flagship.

Successively in later centuries, as all the ships were getting larger, more sail became necessary, which brought with it in turn the appearance of masts made up of various pieces – lower mast, topmast and topgallant mast – which at first were equipped with the sails called the foresail, the

The Pogoria *is another ship, built at the Lenin shipyards in Gdansk between 1979 and 1980, whose rigging could be considered controversial. For historical precision, it may be noted that she was not launched conventionally, but set into the water with a crane (Photo: Javier Sánchez García).*

This Irish brig-schooner, called the Asgard II, *is one of the regular ships at all the tall ship regattas. At the 1996 Cutty Sark, she was chartered for an exclusively female crew (Photo: Javier Sánchez García).*

The Mir *is a modern frigate – although some aspects of her masts and spars are somewhat controversial – built in Poland and virtually identical to the* Pallada, *the* Khersones, *the* Druzhba *and the* Nadeshda *(Photo: Javier Sánchez García).*

The Polish Dar Mlodziezy *is another frigate of the same class as the* Pallada, *the* Mir, *the* Khersones, *the* Druzhba *and the* Nadeshda. *Her name means "Gift of Youth", and her cost was met by public subscription amongst Polish young people (Photo: Javier Sánchez García).*

Part of the Lord Nelson's *crew is not disabled so as to take care of certain manoeuvres. Photograph of a crewmember of this ship climbing the shrouds of the foremast.*

The Eye of the Wind *was built for the South American leather and fur trade. From 1929 she was used for* coastal trading in the Baltic, and in 1995 she starred in the film White Squall.

The Eye of the Wind's *rig makes it easy for her to be mistaken for a square-rig brig because of her two cross masts, although the foremast only has three pieces, and the main a two-part mainsail and only an upper – unfurled – topsail and royal topsail.*

topsail, and the topgallant – on the foremast – mainsail, topsail and topgallant – on the main-mast – and mizzen, mizzen topsail and mizzen topgallant – on the mizzenmast. These would soon have to be folded and multiplied though, due to their increased size and weight. Thus, in the nineteenth century, the clippers were fitted out with a total of almost three dozen sails, and even more on certain occasions, not counting triangular sails or lower studding sails.

In the long and complex evolution of the sailing ship, many different types of rigging appeared, which brought many different names. These include the barque, the brig, the brig-

FOLLOWING PAGE: *The nao* Santa María *on her fifth centenary sailing only with main, fore and mizzen sails during her first trial runs at sea. At that time, the masts were solid pieces and the fore and mizzen masts were only lower pieces.*

Although the Santa María's *sails might seem a little small, one should not be fooled because her yards weigh hundreds of pounds and the rigging she uses is complex and difficult to unfurl. Preparations to raise this ship's mainsail.*

Another view of the nao Santa María, *this time with all her sails hoisted: mainsail, foresail, mizzen sail, topsail and spritsail. Note that the topsail is much more open to the wind than the mainsail and the foresail.*

The Stad Amsterdam *is a reconstruction of a clipper from the tea, gold and wool routes that was built by the cities of Amsterdam and Randstad with the dual purpose of providing work for young tradesmen and serving as a luxury cruise ship.*

Camil Busquets i Vilanova

PREVIOUS PAGE: *The* Stad Amsterdam *can hold a total of 72 passengers in two and four-berth cabins, and up to 125 for day trips, between 80 and 150 for meals and conferences, and between 150 and 300 people for receptions. In the photograph we can see her figurehead.*

In this view of the Stad Amsterdam, *very portside on, two features stand out: the great height of her masts – almost 262 feet high – and her pair of unsinkable, self-righting lifeboats, which are compulsory in compliance with regulations, but nonetheless impair the appearance of the ship.*

BELOW: *The* Stad Amsterdam's *statistics are: displacement, 1,038 t; tonnage, 698 GRT; maximum length, 256 feet; maximum beam, 34,4 feet; draught, 15.74 feet; maximum sail area, 23,680 square feet. It took a total of 300,000 man hours to build this ship.*

PREVIOUS PAGE: *The traditional tall ships, such as this old, painstakingly preserved barque, have a multitude of details that are reminiscent of the most glorious days of nineteenth century sailing (Photo: Javier Sánchez García).*

FOLLOWING PAGE: *Two different details between modern ships and those of years ago. Currently stretching screws tensors are trusted more than lanyards and traditional deadeyes; the belaying pins are made of metal and not wood.*

At the Santander stage of the Cutty Sark 2002, many of the competing ships moored in the Cantabrian capital's port, and there, evocative images such as this one could be seen (Photo: Javier Sánchez García).

In August 2002, in the port of Santander, highly varied types of ships co-existed in friendship and camaraderie, along with crews from many different places (Photo: Javier Sánchez García).

On ships built today we can observe slight differences in the details of their masts and spars. There are subtle differences from the traditional ships mainly due to the use of more sophisticated materials. Close-up of the foremast crosstree on the Baboon.

We may also include ships used for charter in the world of the tall ships and large sailing vessels. In this image we can see the Baboon, *a new ship built in the image and likeness of a veteran brig-schooner.*

FOLLOWING PAGE: *On modern-day ships, one can even find fittings that, regardless of how small the details – such as the modern folding chair on the edge of the picture – could easily pass for traditional fittings.*

The co-existence of traditional systems, devices and materials with more modern ones allows us to combine the practical with the beautiful. Interior view of the gunwale of a modern tall ship, with period details.

The galleon was a transition ship between the nao and the carrack, and one of her prominent features was a forecastle various decks high and one or sometimes two mizzenmasts and many lateen sails. The galleon Every, a replica of a seventeenth century vessel, made from the hull of a Second World War wooden minesweeper.

Although another feature of the galleon was her bowsprit, with the top of storm jib and the yard for the spritsail, or for this and the counter-spritsail, in this photo of the Every *they cannot be seen since she suffered serious damage as the result of a raging storm.*

Polish frigate the Dar Mlodziezy *("Gift of Youth"), thus called because she was donated by public subscription amongst Polish young people. She is a ship from the Syzsza Szkola Morska Gdynia school (Gdynia Naval Academy). Note that the mizzenmast does not have a mizzen sail and only the bare yard can be seen.*

The frigate the Dar Mlodziezy *was built in 1982 in the Lenin shipyards in Gdansk, Poland, and she is virtually identical to other similar ships such as the* Druzhba, *the* Kherones, *the* Mir *and the* Pallada, *which were built on commission for the USSR and currently sail under different flags.*

All these ships have metallic masts, spars and rigging, as do almost all the large modern sailing ships. In the photo, topmen on the frigate Dar Mlodziezy *climbing up the foremast ratlines and shrouds.*

Between 1768 and 1771, the Englishman, James Cook, made an exploratory voyage to the Pacific, discovering new places and drawing maps on board the Endeavour. *Almost three centuries later, a foundation was set up by various entities to reconstruct that ship (Photo: Chris Sattler).*

PREVIOUS PAGE: *This replica of the* Endeavour *was built to celebrate the second centennial of her exploratory voyages (Photo: Chris Sattler).*

In 1994, the Endeavour *repeated her ancestor's voyage (Photo: Chris Sattler).*

The building of this replica of the Endeavour *was funded by the Australian Maritime Museum, with sponsorship by various Australian trusts (Photo: Chris Sattler).*

The Bulgarian brig-schooner Kaliakra *was built at the Paris Commune shipyards in Gdynia, where she was launched on 24th January, 1984, although she was registered at the Lenin shipyards in Gdansk. Her rigging is unique and quite similar to that of the* Pogoria, *with a Marconi mizzen, mainmast with gaff topsail and spanker sail, a large staysail and a foremast with topsails and topgallant sails.*

Aerial view of the Irish Asgard II. *Every year, approximately 500 young Irish people board this ship to learn the art of sailing while gaining important social experience in living together at the same time. She was built in 1981.*

The brig-schooner Kaliakra *took her name from a young Bulgarian heroine who preferred to die rather than fall captive to the Turks in the fourteenth century. Her graceful figure is represented by the ship's figurehead.*

PREVIOUS PAGE: *The square-rig brig* Roald Amundsen *was built in the former East Germany in 1952; between 1990 and 1993 she was reconverted to sail, but her previous design as an oil tanker is clearly seen in the shape of her hull, as may be appreciated in the photo. She belongs to LLAS (LebenLernen auf Segelschiffen e.V).*

schooner, the schooner, the frigate, etc., which on occasions were also used to identify the number of masts used, or the so-called four— or five—mast ships, which evolved from the barque, or the four- or five-mast frigates, becoming the same as the usual frigate. American naval architects even managed to build schooners with seven masts.

The Baltimore clipper called the Pride of Baltimore II, *sailing under most of her sails. This type of ship, extremely fast for the time, was mainly used for guarding the coast and preventing smuggling in nineteenth century America, and as a slave ship as well.*

This highly unusual rig of the Fridtjof Nansen, *a sailing school for young people, which began her life in 1919 as a topsail schooner. Between 1934 and 1981, she became a motor-powered merchant ship by lengthening her hull. In 1981, she was bought to restore her to original rig.*

In the last and perhaps most glorious era of sailing, almost at the point of extinction during the first third of the twentieth century, it was the time of the so-called *windjammers*, sailing ships with a minimum crew and a maximum carrying and load capacity, which were characterised by the enormous extent of their sail area. This was the case of the *Preussen*, the only five-mast frigate that plied the seas until the arrival of the *Royal Clipper*, with a total of 59,847 square feet of sails, slightly smaller than a football pitch or four Olympic-sized pools.

On the *Preussen* everything was superlative. Her displacement was 11,150 t, her total length was 482 feet, with a beam of 53.8 feet and a draught of more than 26 feet. At full sail and with

FOLLOWING PAGE: *The Italian naval training ship* Amerigo Vespucci *is one of the most veteran tall ships still afloat. In the photo, we can see her sailing with fore topsails, topsails, mizzen sails, three jibs, spanker sail and some stay sails.*

The Fridtjob Nansen *is the sail training ship of the Traditionssegler "Fridtjob Nansen" e. V. In the course of her life she has had different names,* Gertrud II *and* Frederik Fischer *(as a sailing ship) and* Edith *(as a motor-powered merchant ship).*

The Russian four-mast ship, the Sedov, *formerly the German* Margaret Vinnen, *is another sailing ship given to Russia as war compensation. She was the largest sailing ship on the high seas.*

The Sedov *(formerly* Margaret Vinnen*) was construction number 372 of the Fried Krupp AG shipyard, where she was built for the Bremen-based company Vinnen F.A. & Co. in 1921. This four-mast barque has a total of 44,670 square feet of sails and reaches a speed of 17 knots under sail only, although she also has an auxiliary engine.*

On the luxury charter tall ships, fittings can be found that would not have been much use on their predecessors. Folding boarding ramp at the stern of the five-mast frigate, Royal Clipper.

The great sailing ships of the nineteenth century had considerable difficulty in careening their hulls. There are currently many types of drydocks and careenages for this purpose.

One area in which the old has succumbed to the new and maximum safety in sailing: communications. Computers, faxes, GPSs, satellite communications... all the latest technology can be found aboard a modern charter tall ship.

A feature that can still be found aboard a tall ship, whether old or modern: the bowsprit and flying jib boom. These triangular sails are only found at the prow and are believed to date from the late eighteenth century; they assist close-hauling.

During the spring of 2000, the Royal Clipper *began operating, for the time being the largest sailing ship in the world, depriving the* Sedov *of this honour. The hull and part of her rigging were built in Danzig, although her masts and spars were finished in Rotterdam.*

One of the most beautiful and charming sailing ships in the world is the four-mast Sea Cloud. *This ship was built in Germany in the 1920s as a yacht for the millionaire, Hutton, who during Second World War ceded it to the US Navy, which converted her into a weather ship.*

At the end of the Second World War, the Sea Cloud *also became the yacht of Generalissimo Trujillo, who re-named her the Patria. In the 1980s, the ship was in a deplorable state in Panama, but she was bought by a German trust, which converted her into a luxury cruise vessel, saving her from being scrapped.*

On the Royal Clipper, *unlike the* Preussen, *all the manoeuvres are mechanical and automatic, so that she is controlled entirely from the pilot bridge deck, with other control consoles for emergencies. In the photo, the main operating console for the rigging on the bridge of the* Royal Clipper.

The Royal Clipper, *just like the* Preussen *long ago, is fitted out with 26 square sails and 16 fore-and-aft sails, with a total sail area of 55,993 feet, which with favourable winds propels her to speeds in the order of 16 knots or even higher. However, to manoeuvre and sail without wind, she has a 4,000 hp diesel engine, with which she reaches speeds of up to 13 knots.*

The frigate Grand Turk, *was built by Mike Turk in Turkey. She represents a 22-cannon British frigate from the end of the eighteenth century to serve as a prop in the TV series on Captain Hornblower (Photo: H & L van Ginderen).*

The frigate Constitution *is commonly and affectionately known as* Old Ironsides. *She entered into service in 1798 and played a major role in the War of 1812 against the British. The US Navy maintains her in service at their base in Norfolk, making a short voyage every 4th July (Photo: H & L van Ginderen).*

One of the most famous sailing ships in history is the Bounty, *on which Fletcher Christian led the mutiny against Captain Bligh. For the filming of a new movie on this subject, a functional replica was built in 1960, which we can see in this photo sailing in the same waters as the original did centuries before (Photo: H & L van Ginderen).*

The Alexander von Humboldt *is a barque built in 1906 and she belongs to the DSST (Deutsche Stiftung Sail Training), and when not sailing, she remains moored in the port of Bremerhaven. Her green sails make her totally unmistakable, just as the large pockets on the crew's jumpsuits make her highly personal (Photo: H & L van Ginderen).*

Curiously, the Royal Clipper *sails under the Luxembourg flag, just like the other ships of the shipbuilder Star Clippers. Since she was built in the image and likeness of the* Preussen, *the only five-mast frigate built until this ship came along, she has similar dimensions.*

The tremendous difference between the Royal Clipper *and the* Preussen *is in the interior, since the latter was a bulk cargo ship and the former one of the most luxurious cruise ships in existence. In the photo, we can see the access stairway to the dining room from the deck where the piano bar is located.*

favourable winds she reached the respectable speed of 17 knots. She was equipped with 46 sails, giving the total sail area stated above. One mast measured a total of 223 feet long, with a circumference of 9.28 feet in the mast hold on deck. One low yard – on the mainmast – measured 103.34 feet long, from one yardarm to the other, and weighed 6.5 t. The entire cordage, added later, would have measured more than 15 miles of steel wire and 10.5 of Manila hemp rope. She had almost 2,296 feet of chains and 1,260 pulleys of various types, from purchases to multiblocks of different types. But she did not use deadeyes because these were replaced by special rigging screws. A low sail weighed between 1,433 and 1,984 pounds, which meant that with its

The cog Ubena von Bremen, *a reconstruction of a Hanseatic boat from the thirteenth to fifteenth centuries. Vessels like this traded between the most important ports in the Baltic Sea, the North Sea and the English Channel, amongst other shores (Photo: H & L van Genderen).*

Years ago and in certain countries interest was aroused in old sailing ships and sailing in the heroic times. Among other replicas in Germany, the Jlieana *was reconstructed; an 18th century cargo ship, seen here in Kiel, in 1993 (Photo: H & L van Genderen).*

cordage and set of blocks and pulleys it came to more than 4,409 pounds, obviously quite a lot for only a dozen topmen.

Nowadays, some of these ships can still be seen, converted into sailing schools, as well as new replicas engaged in pleasure and luxury cruises. But the profitability of these ships is in danger, especially after the travel panic in the USA caused by the terrorist attacks and destruction of the World Trade Center, since we must bear in mind that America's millionaires were the most avid and frequent clients on these vessels.

❑

CHAPTER II

Fore-and-aft rig sailing ships

Modern sport sailing yachts use a few, well-chosen sails that provide excellent performance. One of the most frequently used in sailing is called the spinnaker. The Marconi schooner Oriole *entering Sydney Bay with her spinnaker hoisted (Photo: Chris Sattler).*

II

Fore-and-aft is the term usually used to refer to all rigging that is raised in the bow-to-stern direction on a ship. They are also known as triangular rigs. Thus, according to this definition, there have been numerous fore-and-aft sailboats throughout the ages, since in addition to the current Marconi or Bermuda rigs, with staysails, flying jibs, gaff topsails and lateen sails, triangular sails, lugsails, spritsails and/or dolphin strikers should also be considered fore-and-aft sails.

Triangular rigging turns much better than square rigging, and this is why all ships with square rigging also have fore-and-aft sails, although the opposite is not true. But a large square rig will always need a set of triangular sails since with them it will be able to tack to windward, something that would be quite difficult if it only had its square rigging.

It is worth remembering that a modern regatta yacht fitted out with Marconi rigging (Marconi mainsail, flying jib and/or Genoa) is capable of close turns up to two-quarters, largely depending on the combination of hull/rig – one fourth is 1/32 of the compass, and thus has a value of 11.25 degrees, which means sailing against the wind at an angle of 23 degrees. A square rig would not be able to reach this angle of turn in its wildest dreams. Perhaps the best angle of turn that a square rig could reach is about four-quarters, sometimes less, using its fore-and-aft sails. With only its cross sails, it usually cannot do more than seven quarters. A ship with lateen sails can usually turn between three and four quarters, perhaps closer to the latter. It is believed that the lateen caravels managed to turn up to five or six quarters.

The angle of turn is extremely important in sailing because it is what allows ships to sail against the wind and thus to shorten as much as possible the number of changes in course needed to reach their destination when facing unfavourable winds. So, in ocean sailing, certain routes and winds are always taken advantage of, since, in this way, there is a degree of certainty of making a truly comfortable, easy and brief crossing. Nor does it mean having to make detours, since in a sailing ship it is always more advantageous to lose a certain amount of distance to ensure favourable winds as opposed to exposing oneself to losing these winds or finding unfavourable winds or even no wind at all.

For this reason, the rigging on ocean-going vessels had a certain number of wind sails. And as knowledge of sails, sailing and construction increased, so did the number of triangular sails

The schooner Marconi Karenita *close-hauling with all her rigging: Genoa, mainsail and mizzen sail. She won the Don Juan de Borbón Regatta, in 1993.*

onboard, until what was considered an ideal balance was reached. But the square rigged foresails, spritsail, counter-spritsail and storm jib, so common in the sixteenth and even in the seventeenth century, ended up disappearing, to be replaced by the flying jibs toward the end of the eighteenth century, although at the same time staysails started to be used – bent over a stay – and the mizzen lateen sail – several of which were used at a time on the same or different masts – ended up being exchanged for a single spanker sail.

The evolution of the spanker sail is interesting in itself, since first it lost the fore part of the sail, and then later ended up losing the 'dry' part of the lateen yard. It is said that cutting off the fore part happened by chance, when the mizzen lateen sail of a galleon split and the captain rein-

International 49 feet class yacht, Tuiga. *Large sailing yachts of this type are almost the sole survivors of the most glorious era of sport yachting, when the America's Cup served to streamline the design and construction of large yachts to the utmost.*

forced the split part on the mast so that it would not get in the way. This resulted in the consequent surprise when he saw the improved effectiveness. With regard to the spanker sail, it is also interesting that frigates are equipped with a spanker sail on their mizzenmast. Sometimes the mizzen sail gets in the way of the wind reaching. And given that for manoeuvring, the former is more important than the latter, some captains systematically refused to unfurl the mizzen sail, leaving it always tied to its yard. From that to bending it was a simple step. The yard though, no longer carrying sail, became redundant. It was not removed from the frigates however, because the sheet tacks of the mizzen sail were attached to that yard. And virtually the same could be said about the square-rigged spanker, although in this case it was the main topsail.

PREVIOUS PAGE: *The* Tuiga *was built at Fairlie, UK in 1909, commissioned by the Duke of Mendinaceli to compete in Spanish regattas with His Majesty, King Alfonso XIII. This ship was painstakingly restored in the 1980s and can be considered a jewel of naval architecture.*

FOLLOWING PAGE: *The barque,* James Craig, *in January, 1998, after launching with her hull totally restored and only the lower masts and a makeshift rig. This ship was one of the favourites at the Sydney Olympics, and she appears on the lists of the Sydney Heritage Fleet, at the Sydney Maritime Museum (Photo: Chris Sattler).*

In 1874, the barque James Craig *started to sail, one of the many sailing ships at that time. Through many twists of fate, she managed to survive a long life and was acquired at the end of the 1990s by the Sydney Naval Museum for restoration. In the photo, we can see her with a makeshift rig, just after her restoration launching, in 1998 (Photo: Chris Sattler).*

The schooner rig is one of the most elegant and fastest in existence, and was thus chosen by the pilots of many ports, so it is also known as a Pilot Boat. In the photo we can see the Freda *during a period boat regatta.*

With few exceptions, ships rigged exclusively with triangular sails are usually smaller than the imposing square-rigged tall ships. A delightful schooner in which wood plays an important role.

If her hull is made of wood and is to be maintained in perfect conditions for sailing, a small yacht also requires proper maintenance.

Keeping a large sailboat in service, regardless of its size, means periodic maintenance work which on occasions can involve almost total reconstruction.

Replacing plank strakes and caulking joints are quite frequent operations on a wooden-hulled ship, besides being absolutely essential.

The ketch Mingary *was built in 1929, by Bute Slip Dock Company in Scotland, using iroko, oak and teak wood. With a length of 68 feet, she can hold five passengers in her two cabins. At the end of 2001, she was put on sale for approximately 140,000 £.*

The Asgard II *is an Irish brig-schooner, built in 1981, and fitted out by the government itself. In this view, she is close-hauling with most of her fore-and-aft rig.*

Colombus' caravels were at first outfitted with lateen sails, although they were later partially re-rigged with square rigging, still keeping the lateen sails on the mizzenmast. The nao Santa María, *built to commemorate the 500th anniversary of the discovery of America, sailing only with mizzen and foresails.*

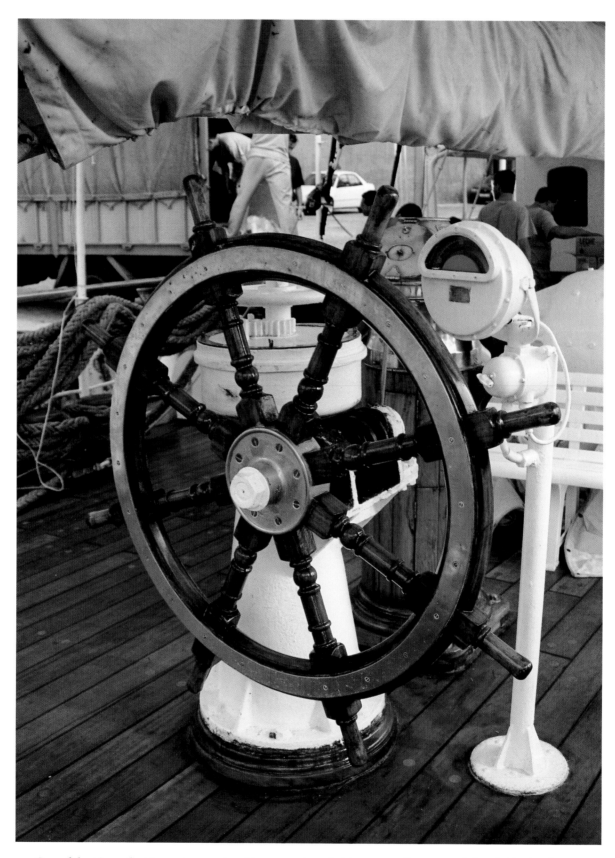

One of the pieces that is most appreciated by souvenir and ship-parts collectors, and for which significant amounts are paid, is the helm wheel.

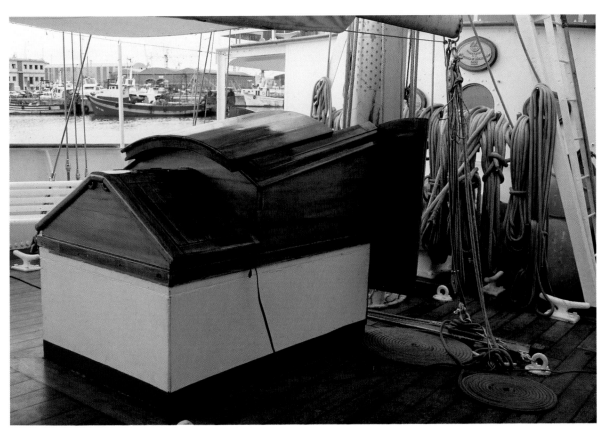

On certain large sailing ships, wood and steel co-exist everywhere. An unusual hatchway house aboard the Uruguayan navy training ship Capitán Miranda.

In some countries and/or regions coasters were highly considered as they supplied the small coastal towns for many centuries before the arrival of rail and road transport (Photo: Javier Sánchez García).

The compass is the most highly valued tool by helmsman for maintaining the ship's course. The ancient Vikings are believed to have made use of a primitive form of the compass for guiding their ships at sea (Photo: Javier Sánchez García).

The dinghy – the smallest of the tenders aboard a ship – of a large sailing ship can be stowed on deck or, as shown here, hung from davits on the stern, ready for lowering.

The safety required by international regulations calls for all on-board tackle to be reeved as effectively as possible. Shroud lanyards/deadeyes alongside backstays and other ropes. Note the stainless steel thimbles and shackles (Photo: Javier Sánchez García).

On the outside of the hull of the tall ships there are many different types of tackle, such as these blocks that probably form part of the set of mast braces (Photo: Javier Sánchez García).

On sailing ships of a certain size, on each side of the wheelhouse are the so-called repeaters, which are used to take certain measurements and check locations (Photo: Javier Sánchez García).

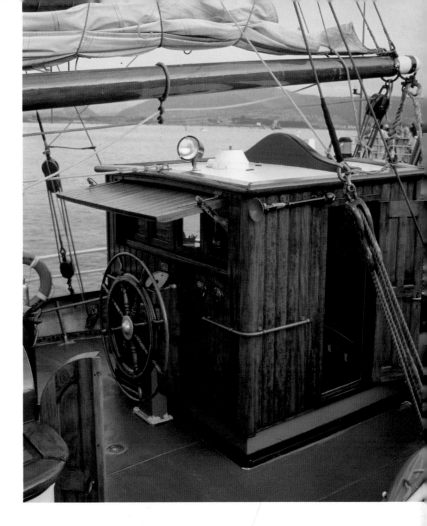

The position of the helm wheel can at times lead to confusion, as the helmsman apparently has to pilot the ship with his back turned, although this is not so since he usually stands sideways on (Photo: Javier Sánchez García).

Mechanical propulsion requires fittings such as the typical funnel – in explosion engines a simple outlet for fumes to escape, usually associated with a skylight and the ventilation and lighting shafts for the engine room (Photo: Javier Sánchez García).

FOLLOWING PAGE: *The Frankish schooner, known as the pilot boat, is usually found with fore-and-aft or triangular rigging. In the photo, the* Tho-Pa-Ga, *formerly* Tres Hermanos *and* Cala Tuent *was built in the 1920s.*

The pilot boat, Tho-Pa-Ga, *formerly the* Cala Tuent *and before that the* Tres Hermanos, *was built in 1918 at a Murcia boatyard. In the Cádiz-2000 Regatta she was re-named* ONO/City of Cádiz *and was the city's ambassador at the various ports used in the regatta.*

FOLLOWING PAGE: *Since 1987, the four-mast Portuguese schooner* Creoula *has been a sail training school for the Portuguese navy. She was built in 1936 and was used for fishing the Newfoundland banks for almost 40 years.*

The so-called schooner rig has undergone major changes throughout history, with many different types in existence. In the photo, there is a slightly unusual schooner with stay sails, which represented the Autonomous Community of Valencia at the Cádiz-2000 regatta.

PREVIOUS PAGE: *The so-called whaling boat is a dinghy that started to be used aboard the whaling ships and it is where the whales were harpooned from. Her main external feature is that she does not have a square stern (Photo: Javier Sánchez García).*

The so-called 'bou' is a fishing vessel that originally fished in pairs, a type of fishing in which two identical boats dragged the net to keep it open. This is the Alzina, a 'mizzen bou' sailing into the wind with three reef bands.

The Arung Samudera *(formerly* Adventurer*) is a three-mast schooner built in New Zealand in 1996. She hoists a total of 4,669.3 square feet sail and is the training ship for the Indonesian navy.*

In 1900, the novelist Joseph Conrad published Lord Jim, *a novel of maritime adventures. This schooner with staysails bears the name of the main character of the book.*

PREVIOUS PAGE: *Not all navies have large sailing ships as schools. The Belgian navy uses the ketch* Zenobe Gramme *for this purpose, a ship that for some time also carried out oceanic explorations.*

The topsail schooner Volchitsa *beating windward in the 1993 period ship regatta. This ship sank at the end of that decade in waters off the Canary Islands on a charter cruise. Fortunately there were no victims.*

The Russian topsail schooner Volchitsa. *Her* rara avis *spanker sail is worth noting since it is not bent over the mast. This ship was built in the 1990s near Saint Petersburg and for several years was engaged in charter trips.*

Another 'redundant' yard, although it was removed some time after the arrival of the flying jibs, is the one used formerly for the spritsail. This sail was used in an attempt to improve ships' pitching. Due to its location, however, they used to take on quite a bit of water, and ships had to be provided with scuppers to eliminate all the water taken on board during pitching.

There are rigs that are somewhat complex and difficult to classify. Such is the case of this interesting and unusual vessel which hoists two lateen sails and two flying jibs, all of them truly exceptional.

A triangular sail that is usually associated with the presence of spanker sails is the so-called gaff topsail, a triangular sail which is hoisted to the top of the mast and tied down at the stern onto the spanker sail gaff. This sail is usually only hoisted when the wind and course are duly established. It remains to one side of the halyard of the topsail gaff, so, when one wants to change tack, the tack line and kicking strap have to be passed over it; a manoeuvre that often ends in people being sent up to the crosstree, which is always a risky business.

One of the best-known fore-and-aft sails, especially in the Mediterranean, is the so-called lateen. This sail is considered older than the other existing sails, and it is believed that it was brought to the Mediterranean by the Arabs, possibly from the Indian Ocean. Its name comes from a corruption – *a la trina* – referring to its triangular shape, and has nothing to do, as has

FOLLOWING PAGE: *The Italian Navy currently has two ships used as sailing schools, one of which is the brig-schooner* Palinuro, *a cod boat used on the great fishing banks, which was launched in 1934 in Nantes. She was bought by the Navy in 1951 to serve as its sailing school for petty officers and is registered at the base in La Maddalena, Sardinia.*

been mentioned several times, with the Romans, since they did not even use it. Except for the Marconi, it is considered the best sail for beating windward and sailing crosswind, although it performs worse than the square rig when sailing with tailwinds.

One of special features of this type of sail is that, even though possible, due to the considerable difficulty of changing it on board and given that to do so a long lateen yard has to be passed behind the mast, the ship is usually sailed with the sail on the same side, which produces the unusual effect of double or single pocketing, depending on which side the wind is blowing. This is called "good" or "in favour of the tree" when the wind comes from the side the mast is on, and "bad" or "against the tree" if it comes from the other side.

Vessels with two lateen sails, such as xebecs, feluccas and certain galleys, are sometimes sailed goose-wing. The lateen yards lie opposite in different directions and lean out behind the horizon, producing an effect similar to that of two donkey's ears. This way of sailing is also used on schooners when its spanker sails open up on both sides.

The rigging known as Bermuda or Marconi is the type most frequently found on yachts and

The packet boat Rafael Verdera. *She is also considered a tartane. This is the oldest ship preserved in Spain. She was built in the middle of the nineteenth century on Majorca, and on one occasion was the target of the wrath of Catalan independence groups, who tried to burn her through mistaking her for the nao* Santa María.

The Rafael Verdera *used an interesting and unusual rig, which some people considered to be more characteristic of a packet boat than of a tartane. In any case, she has a fore-and-aft rig that enables her to sail reasonably, although she is an old veteran ship with more than a century and a half behind her.*

The spinnaker is a very strange sail that is only used in tailwinds, having to be lowered for crosswinds and close-hauls. It is a little complicated to define whether it is a square or fore-and-aft sail. It is fitted out on a special boom and is usually extraordinarily brightly coloured. It is sometimes even used for advertising.

cutters built from the end of the nineteenth century and throughout the twentieth century. Their main feature is that they are fastened directly to the mast and gaff sail boom by means of cringles, with a peculiar position and distribution of shrouds and crosstrees. It somewhat resembles the original wireless telegraph antennae, which is where the name Marconi rigging comes from. Their special qualities when beating windward have made them the favourite sails of all competitive and/or leisure crafts, although the height of their masts make them less common on larger ships.

The term "Bermuda" is applied due to the fact that they come from the Bermuda Islands, although, just like everything, this does not appear to be a completely sure explanation and others are thrown in. In any event, what is certain is that, in 1796, a book by David Steele entitled *Practice of Sailmaking* was published in London and made reference to a sail called the "shoulder

The ketch led to the yawl, which is characterised by having its mizzenmast in the rake of stern. Although not very common, it is not exceptional either, as is the case of this boat we see in the photo.

The Genoa sail began to be used in the 1920s and took its name because it was first used in that city. It is a large flying jib whose sheet tack is behind the mast.

Sometimes, little jokes are made in yacht racing. Such is the case of this German-registered schooner with spanker sails christened Bla Jungfru, *which hoists the feared pirate Jolly Roger along with the EU flag.*

A schooner with a fore-and-aft rig of spankers and flying jibs can sail close to the wind, although less so than with Marconi sails. The topmasts, in this case, are probably trimmed, so that it is impossible to hoist spanker sails.

The so-called cutter used to only hoist a spanker sail with gaff topsail and some flying jibs, sometimes a topsail as well on larger vessels. This obviously is not the case with the vessel we see in this photo.

A Marconi ketch with Genoa and flying jib. These days this rig is quite common, especially on larger ships. She beats into the wind well and allows one to sail comfortably and safely.

FOLLOWING PAGE: *Sometimes hulls have unusual shapes to be equipped with masts and different sails; such is the case of this ketch with spanker sails whose stern reveals an origin far removed from sporting use.*

This slightly Saracen-looking vessel is fitted out with rather unusual sails, with a lateen-like appearance although with a one-piece metal lateen yard, which at the same time serves as a mast from a socket brace on the deck.

The pilot boat Santa Eulalia *is a floating extension of the Maritime Museum of the Royal Shipyards in* Barcelona. *The restoration of this ship was quite complicated since she was built as the* Carmen Flores *at a Torrevieja boatyard shortly after the First World War.*

PRECEDING PAGE: *On shorter boats the lateen sail adapts better than one of the more common mainsail and flying jib rigs, although in this case the sail is still a slightly unusual lateen judging by certain details reminiscent of the so-called settle sail.*

During its long life afloat, the Santa Eulalia *was originally the* Carmen Flores, *then the* Puerto de Palma, *followed by the* Cala San Vicens, *and finally the* Sayremar I. *As the* Cala San Vicens *she was converted into a motor sailboat, and as the* Sayremar I *into a marine recovery and salvage boat.*

PREVIOUS PAGE: *Although the features of lateen sails differ somewhat depending on the wind and whether they form a single pocket or not, the lateen yard is rarely changed to leeward with the sole objective of increasing these features. An "against the tree" lateen sail.*

With the masts and spars completed, the main part of the salvage and restoration of the Santa Eulalia *was finished. In the photo we can see her with her tackle and ropes totally ready and waiting to receive her sails.*

Teaching sailing is a constant feature of navies and merchant marines, since sailing is considered the best school to prepare for any type of navigation. In the picture, the Portuguese navy's sailing school the Vega.

FOLLOWING PAGE: *The Baltimore clipper was a very fast ship that plied the coasts of the USA. In this picture we can see the* Pride of Baltimore II *sailing with her two spanker sails and small jib. One of the most noteworthy characteristics of this type of ship is the considerable slope of her masts.*

In the history of sailing there have been many different types of ships and vessels used by man. Sailboats from two opposing worlds: a Chinese junk with her unusual matting sails with which she sails on any course, and a spanker sail schooner at close-haul (Photo: H & L van Ginderen).

The caravel was the ocean-exploring vessel par excellence, used particularly by the Spanish and Portuguese. The Portuguese lateen sail caravel the Boa Esperança built in 1930. Interestingly, she is sailing "against the tree"
(Photo: H & L van Ginderen).

of mutton", which was quite similar to the Bermuda. Another explanation goes that, in 1808, a born loser in all competitions appeared in one regatta with a sail of this type, beating his competitors hands down, who immediately wante to know what the secret of his success was. But there is also the story of a schooner that plied the seas between Hamilton and the shipyard on the island of Ireland, in the Bermudas. As a result of the constant bother of hoisting and lowering the sails from the spanker sail gaff, someone came up with the idea of trimming the sails and eliminating the gaff, thus obtaining greater turning capacity.

And that is not all since there still exist a few more versions with regard to the origin of the Marconi sail. In any case, one can be sure that this type of sail, along with its current system of

The Dutch built a large maritime colonial empire using ships such as this one. A replica of the Amsterdam, *an eighteenth century Flemish cargo galleon, sailing only with the mizzen sail and a flying jib (Photo: H & L van Ginderen).*

The brig-schooner Mercator, *which we see here heaving to with most of its fore-and-aft sails is a modern vessel built in steel, including her spars and masts (Photo: H & L van Ginderen).*

bending and masts, makes it extraordinarily aerodynamic, especially since its design and cut, regardless of its sewing, still carried out by hand, are done using CAD/CAM computer systems, with the result pocketing and deformations are optimised to the utmost. Hence the extraordinary benefits it offers, such as those of the sails on a modern America's Cup yacht, or one of the large catamarans that sailed around the world without supply stops in The Race regatta held in January and February, 2001, at the turn of the millennium.

❏

CHAPTER III

Regattas, meets and cruises

Tall ship enthusiasts seriously enjoy their gatherings and regattas, since they have the chance to view a large number of these ships. In the photo, a jungle of masts and yards in the port of Cádiz at the Cádiz-2000 Regatta.

III

The costs of maintaining a large sailing ship nowadays are only within the reach of navies, sailing schools and cultural associations and foundations. However, there is another possibility reserved only for the very wealthy: super luxury cruises on board tall ships. There is also a cheaper option: embarking on a ship that admits passengers, although also serving as part-time crew member, since passengers are encouraged to participate in the on-board tasks. This, however, calls for you to have certain sailing skills and/or to be in good physical shape.

As a result, the few large-sized sailing vessels – also known as the tall ships – are ships that are not common on the seas and tend to be reserved for the most favourable seasons. After all, we are not trying to re-create the exploits of the great explorers but to enjoy a few days' sailing and camaraderie. Since a cruise ship is for pleasure, clearly the most common thing is to offer the passengers an unforgettable journey, but one that is unforgettable because of the setting and not because of experiences reminiscent of the worst moments that any ocean-faring explorer might have undergone.

Yet, since the costs of amortising a ship of this type are high, on the super luxury cruise ships voyages are usually planned in accordance with the setting and the time of year, usually taking place in the summer in the Mediterranean or Baltic Seas, and in the winter along the coasts of the Caribbean islands or Florida.

With sailing ships, one must always err on the side of caution and be very aware of unfortunate, tragic events such as the loss of the *Pamir*, a sailing school and four-mast ship flying the West German flag, which sank near the Azores because of a typhoon on the 21st September, 1957, in which 80 young lives were lost out of the total crew of 86 men.

Almost every summer, when the favourable winds and seas arrive, there are many different sailing regattas and meets, some of which have gained international fame and are more highly considered among the usual participants. This point can be proven by a translation of the well-known Spanish maritime saying: "July, August and Mahon are the best ports in the Mediterranean".

When many large sailing ships come to the gatherings, they are usually requested to moor alongside one other, inevitably resulting in the masts overlapping and details getting confused. Foremasts of the Eye of the Wind *and the* Lord Nelson.

At the Cádiz-2000 Regatta, in the region of a dozen large tall ships and almost twice that number of other smaller ships gathered together. A line of hulls and masts and spars along the Reina Victoria and Marqués de Comillas docks.

Aerial view of the port of Cádiz during the departure of the Great Cádiz-2000 Regatta. The Gorch Fock *can be seen in the exit channel and the* Amerigo Vespucci *and* Juan Sebastián de Elcano *can be seen still moored on the Ciudad de Cádiz dock, with the Russian* Mir *at the end of the dock along with the oceanographic research ship the* Hesperides.

CHARTER AND PLEASURE SAILING

From day to day, the opportunity of embarking on a tourist pleasure cruise in a period ship – or one that looks like a period ship – is becoming more possible, especially since the appearance of two brand-new ships, the *Royal Clipper* and the *Stad Amsterdam*. Until recently, this was only possible on board the *Sea Cloud*, a truly old ship.

There are also other more modern sailing ships used for these purposes, with totally modern appearances, although this is not considered very attractive by some people. These include the *Club Med 1* and *2*; the *Star Clipper* and *Star Flyer*; and the *Wind Star, Wind Song, Wind Spirit* and

The moment of departure, surrounded by all types of vessels full of spectators, of the Great Cádiz-2000 Regatta. From left to right we see the Spanish pilot boat Tho-Pa-Ga/Ciudad de Cádiz, *the barque* Europa *and the frigate* Dar Mlodziezy.

Wind Surfer. All of them are quite similar in terms of their features and services, especially the first two and last four, which are even similar in size and external appearance.

The *Sea Cloud* is a super luxury yacht, with a four-mast rig, built in Germany in the first quarter of the last century. She belonged to the millionaire Hutton and the dictator Trujillo. The *Royal Clipper* is a working replica of the only five-mast frigate that ever existed, the *Preussen*, an exceptional ship by all accounts. The *Stad Amsterdam* is also a copy of a clipper from the tea route designed, like the other ships, as a floating luxury hotel. The *Star Clipper* and the *Star Flyer* were built *ex novo* in Europe as floating hotels, but with modified rigging to be guided via computers, more or less similar to the *Winds* quartet.

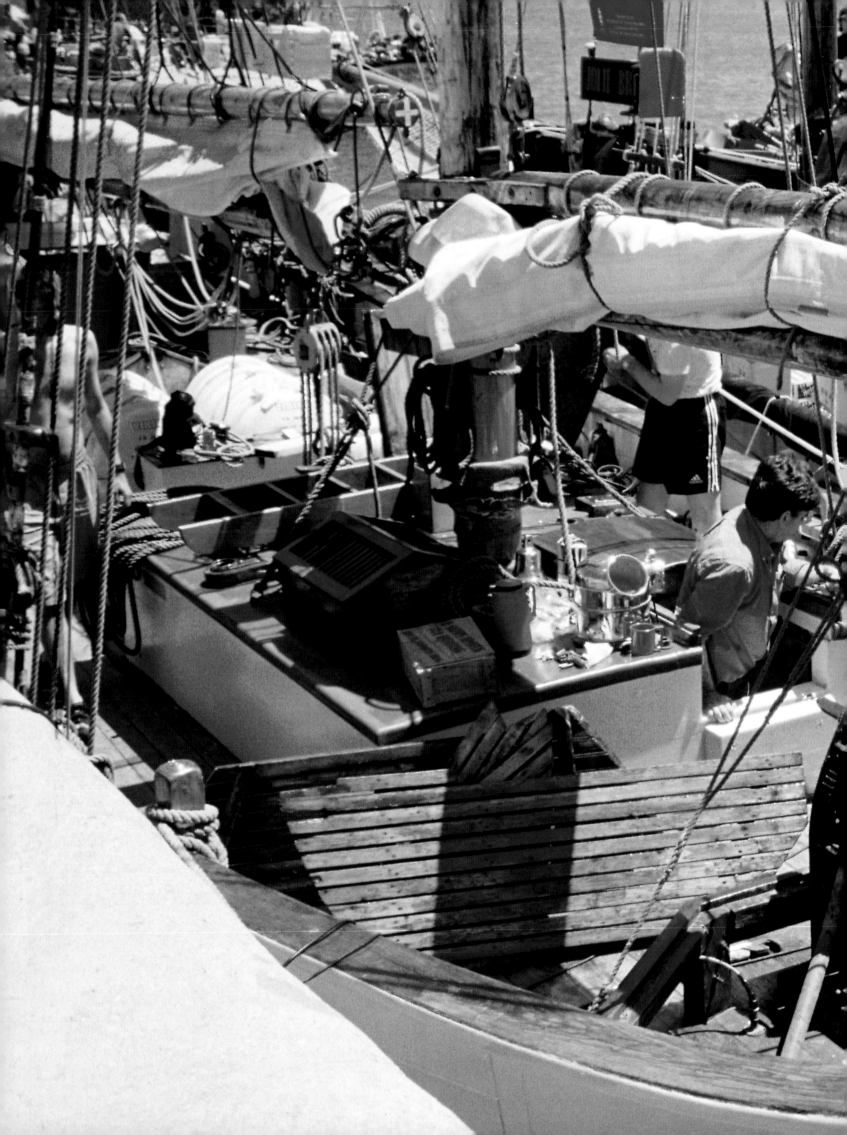

PREVIOUS PAGE: *At certain meetings and times it is possible to admire the details of a number of tall ships. A partial view of a schooner with spanker sails, with the poop deck, the spanker boom and main spanker sail gaff in the first place.*

At a less luxurious level, but undoubtedly also valid in terms of nautical and sailing criteria, we should also mention other large sailing ships, many of them sailing schools, which does not stop them from admitting civil passengers on board at times. Such is the case of the ships *Dar Mlodziezy, Druzjba, Khersones, Mir, Hadhezdha* and *Pallada*, to which two more names should be added, the *Kruzenshtern* and the *Sedov*, both from the 1920s and the last of the windjammers still preserved.

THE CUTTY SARK TALL SHIPS' RACE

In 1954, a retired London lawyer named Bernard Morgan had the idea of organising an annual regatta with the aim of recalling the most glorious period of sailing. Its organisation is rather unusual, since the quickest ship does not win, rather the crew that by popular vote is believed to have done the most for fraternisation and friendship among the ships during that regatta. The trophy consists of a silver replica of the clipper Cutty Sark.

The moment of departure of the Great Cádiz-2000 Regatta, surrounded by all types of vessels, from left to right, the Russian Kruzenshtern, *the German* Gorch Fock *and the Spanish* Juan Sebastián de Elcano, *among others.*

The Roald Amundsen *alongside the* Europa *during the Cádiz-2000. The former belongs to the Learn to Live on Sailing Ships Association, and both of them welcome on board volunteers who wish to learn to sail and live together with young people from all over the world.*

The Indonesian sailing school brig-schooner Dewarutji *arriving at Sydney Harbour with her crew having climbed the spars and masts to pay honours. The ship was built in 1953, in Germany (Photo: Chris Sattler).*

PREVIOUS PAGE: *The frigate* Pallada *entering Sydney Harbour. She was built by Stocznia in Poland, in Gdansk in 1989. Along with the* Druzhba, *the* Kherzones, *the* Mir, *and the* Dar Mlodziezy *she is one of a uniform group (Photo: Chris Sattler).*

The pilot boat Tho-Pa-Ga, *the former* Tres Hermanos *and* Cala Tuent. *She was built at the boatyards at Águilas, Murcia, Spain, in 1924. For almost 60 years, she was engaged in plying the ports along the east coast of Spain before being bought by a French citizen who has restored and maintains her.*

The Mexican navy training barque Cuauhtemoc *was built in Spain by Astilleros y Talleres Celaya. Here, we can see her with her crew lining the yards in a salute to the Australian city of Sydney (Photo: Chris Sattler).*

In a regatta of period ships, in this case the Don Juan de Borbón/Almirante Conde de Barcelona, a great many vessels with interesting rigs attend. A spanker sail sloop with her gaff topsail hoisted.

The Russian four-mast ship, the Kurzenshtern, *starting out on the Great Cádiz-2000 Regatta under full sail with the exception of her spanker sails and gaff topsail.*

A moment during the period ship regatta Don Juan de Borbón. The ketch Gipsy *with her mixed fore-and-aft sails made up of a Marconi mainsail, a mizzen spanker sail and two good-sized jibs.*

PREVIOUS PAGE: *Undoubtedly, one of the most famous vessels in history was the schooner the* America, *which paved the way for the America's Cup, the most famous regatta for sailing ships. In the photo, a replica of this ship.*

FOLLOWING PAGE: *The chaos of ropes, chains, sails, yards and masts is notable in this detailed view of the top of the mast of the barque* Europa.

The Russian training barque the Kruzenshtern *moored at one of the docks in Cádiz during its Great Regatta.*

PREVIOUS PAGE: *In her day, the* Amerigo Vespecci *had a virtual twin in the* Cristóforo Colombo. *This ship, given to Russia at the end of the Second World War, was lost in the Black Sea in unknown and somewhat mysterious circumstances.*

The large sailing ships have attractive, elegant details in every corner of their anatomy. Helm wheel on the barque Europa.

The Gorch Fock *is also one of the most elegant tall ships, and she is one of the most frequently seen at regattas and meetings. She is the second ship of this name owned by the German navy, since the first was also handed over to Russia, where she was re-named the* Tovaritsch.

The Kurzenshtern *was one of the last windjammers to sail. She was built in Germany in 1926, as the* Padua. *She was requisitioned by Russia at the end of the war and is currently the sail training ship of the Russian Fishing Academy, which is based in Kaliningrad, the former Prussian Königsburg.*

The figurehead is one of the great constants to be seen on all sailing vessels, and some are true works of art by renowned sculptors and artisans. The figurehead of the Palinuro, with this figure of Palinurus, the helmsman of Aeneas.

Another part of the tall ships which tends to have ornamentation is the stern, especially the escutcheon and the crown. Detail of the escutcheon of the topsail schooner Volchitsa.

A great deal of ornamentation and luxury could be found on the sterns of some galleons, and it is said that at times their richness was so great that capturing one meant that the captor's fortune was made. The galleon Neptuno *was reproduced in striking detail, but she is all made of fibreglass, plastic and paint.*

PREVIOUS PAGE: *On seventeenth, eighteenth and nineteenth century ships there was an area over the stem that was constantly lashed by waves when the boat pitched back and forth. The lavatories were sometimes placed there, since the seawater washed them out continually.*

The galleon was a ship that evolved from the nao. She was typical of the sixteenth and seventeenth centuries, and gold, silver, fabrics, spices and other great fortunes were transported on her. In the photo, a replica of a galleon from around the seventeenth century used as background scenery in the movie Pirates.

Maintenance of a period ship is complicated since they are ships with a wooden hull, whose strakes must be changed frequently and kept perfectly caulked in order to preserve the wood.

In the Cutty Sark Tall Ships' Race, as many sailing ships can take part as wish to, without any other restriction than that they are longer than 29 feet, and that half of their crew be made up of young people between the ages of 16 and 25.

The first Cutty Sark race was held in 1956, and it gathered together 21 sailing ships from 11 countries which sailed from Torbay to Lisbon. The number of participants has increased since 1972, when the regatta was in danger of disappearing due to financial difficulties. Sponsorship by the firm Berry, Bros & Rudd, owners of the whisky brand Cutty Sark, solved the problem and ever since then they have been the sponsors, commissioning the International Sail Training Association with organising it. In the region of over fifty ships have gathered together in the most recent Cutty Sark races.

The Sir Robert Baden Powell *is a topsail schooner built in 1956 that usually makes charter voyages in the waters of the Caribbean and the Balearic Islands. She has seven comfortable double cabins, some of which can accommodate three people.*

Each year at the end of summer at the traditional village of Cadaqués on Spain's Costa Brava, there is a very popular meeting of lateen sail vessels, frequently attended by boats from the ports of Southern France.

The vessels that take part in the period regattas show painstakingly cared-for details from a historical or technical point of view. Close view of the foot of the main mast on the Pride of Baltimore II.

PREVIOUS PAGE: *It is also common for the interiors of reconstructed ships to preserve similar degrees of historical and technical details, which are sometimes used by interior designers as a source of inspiration. Cabin on the* Pride of Baltimore II.

COMMEMORATIVE REGATTAS

Commemorative regattas are organised in order to celebrate an important anniversary, generally discoveries, a country's independence, or the end of a war.

Without a doubt, the most important tall ship regatta ever celebrated was that marking the 500th anniversary of the discovery of the New World, called Colón-92, in which different participating ships set sail from Cádiz, Spain on the 3rd May, covering the course from Cádiz to New York (Cádiz – Canary Islands – San Juan, Puerto Rico – New York) and Boston, from where they weighed anchor on the 16th July, bound for Liverpool, in an

It was a lost opportunity for Spain, but not for the United Kingdom. Hull of the barque Galatea *before its move to Seville, where not even the many millions spent by that city in Expo-92 were enough to save her. Acquired at the price of scrap by the British, she now lies in the Port of Glasgow, totally restored.*

FOLLOWING PAGE: *In order to reduce their crews, the windjammers used high powered, somewhat sophisticated winches to simultaneously reeve all the braces on the same mast. Detail of the deck of the* Sedov, *where these winches can be seen amongst other items.*

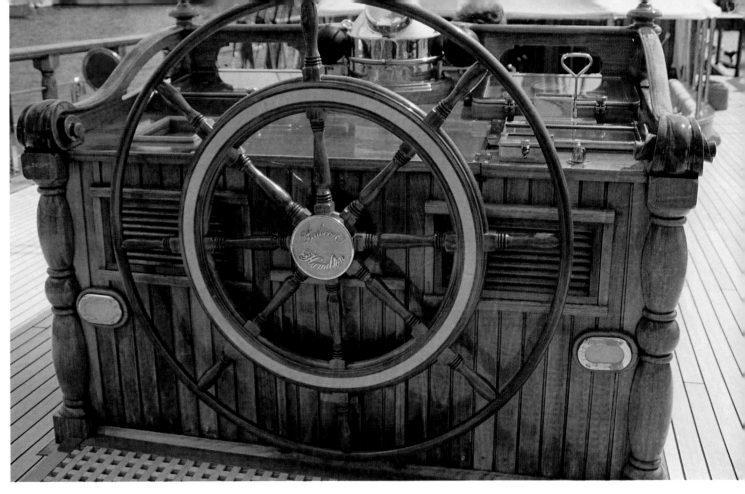

The Baboon *is a probable topsail schooner which, like many other sailing ships currently on the seas, makes charter voyages to various locations. A close view of the command post on this ship.*

PREVIOUS PAGE: *Although the tackle on windjammers is simplified as far as possible, using among other things special rigging screws instead of deadeyes and lanyards, it is still quite complicated. Detail of the main foremast of the Sedov.*

On sailing ships that make luxury charter trips it is usual to find highly decorative details in extremely good taste. A bench built into the command post on the poop deck of the Baboon.

The Barcelona yachting marina Port Vell periodically houses sailing ships for luxury charter cruises and/or private vessels of all types and sizes. The topsail schooner Baboon *moored at the Port Vell marina, in the port of Barcelona.*

Even when recently built ships attempt to achieve the greatest verisimilitude in the technical and historical aspects of older ships, there are always certain occasions on which practical, pragmatic solutions are adopted in order to ease manoeuvring capabilities. Close view of the foremast of a modern sailing ship.

PREVIOUS PAGE: *The* Star Clipper *is a beautiful sailing ship with a modern design and construction, built in Ghent, by the Belgium Shipbuilders Corp, in 1990. She belongs to the company Star Clippers, a specialist in luxury sailing cruises (Photo: Star Clippers).*

The Star Flyer *is* Star Clipper's *twin, built one year before at the same shipyards. In the photo, we can see her arriving at the Port of Barcelona in 1992, to be used as a floating hotel during the Olympics held in the city in the summer of that year.*

During the 1992 Olympics, the Port of Barcelona received the visit of various luxury cruise sailing ships which were used as floating hotels. In the photo, the Star Flyer *at that time housed the staff of Audi, just like the* Sea Cloud, *which we can also see moored at the same dock fully stern on, which housed the staff of that other celebrated automobile company, Mercedes Benz.*

PREVIOUS PAGE: *At the ports of call and intermediate stopovers in the sailing regattas, there is always time for a moment of relaxation, camaraderie and fraternisation between one working session and the next.*

The poop deck is considered the ship's 'noble' area, where the most luxurious wood and decoration can be found. Poop deck on the Europa *with the cabin skylights and deck benches.*

FOLLOWING PAGE: *For sailors and enthusiasts, the great tall ships' ports of call are an opportunity to study and compare different types of rigging since there are always some that are more unorthodox than others.*

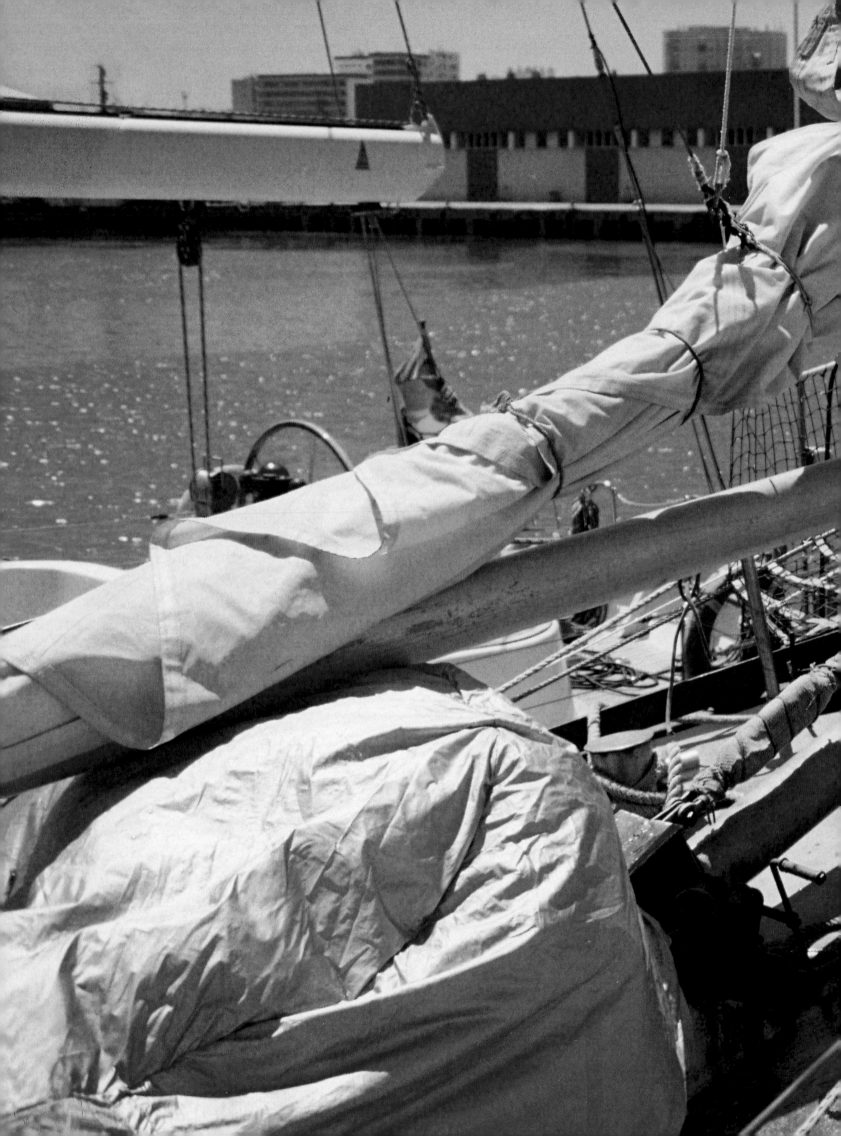

PREVIOUS PAGE: *Tiller control of the rudder still exists on board certain ships, especially smaller-sized ones, although the helm wheel is usually preferred whenever possible (Photo: Javier Sánchez García).*

At the beginning of the twenty-first century The Race, the so-called Regatta of the Century, was held, in which ships went round the world under sail power alone. A large-scale advertising campaign was conducted for this race. In the photo, the moment of departure at Barcelona's Olympic Port.

The ships used in The Race were all maxi-catamarans or VLMHs (Very Large Multi-Hull), a highly sophisticated type of boat which has an appearance that is often more reminiscent of a space craft than a yacht.

The hulls of the maxi-catamarans are extremely long and narrow, with angled rudders to control the vessel better when listing. Due to the risks involved in their voyages, all the boats are fitted out with latest-technology communication systems.

If these ships seem narrow when viewed from aft, from the bow they look like razor blades. Their crews, reduced in number and very carefully selected, are made up of true athletes who adjust the rigging by walking over a net that also serves as a deck.

One of the almost "secret weapons" of the maxi-catamarans are their sliding centreboards, which can be regulated in draught so that their sailing qualities are improved considerably.

PREVIOUS PAGE: *Along with the hull, the most important item on a maxi-catamaran is the mast. With profiles carefully studied in wind tunnels and built using the most advanced space technology and the latest generation composites, the mast on one of these great sailboats is capable of bending without breaking, even in extreme conditions... providing that it is properly braced.*

One of the top favourites in The Race, at least on paper, was Steve Fosset's Play Station. *However, his mediocre results led him to retire before reaching the mid-Atlantic.*

Occasionally, special crews are prepared for some of the main tall ship regattas. This is the case of the Eye of the Wind, *which sailed with an all female crew in the 1996 Cutty Sark.*

FOLLOWING PAGE: *One of the special features the tall ships, especially those built in the nineteenth century, was the figurehead, some of which had true value as sculptures, besides others that acquired legendary status (Photo: Javier Sánchez García).*

In some cases on board a large sailing ship one can find figures that are not always identified as figureheads – the figurehead is always located at the upper end of the stem – although they certainly do not cease to have a charm all their own (Photo: Javier Sánchez García).

Among figureheads, along with graceful and refined ladies, there are fierce, bearded warriors, as well as animals and floral motifs (Photo: Javier Sánchez García).

PREVIOUS PAGE: *At the different stages of any tall ship regatta, views of jungles of masts and rigging are commonplace, always a first-rate spectacle, besides evoking memories of former times.*

Although all ships look alike to the uninitiated, for enthusiasts all sailing vessels both great and small have their own special charm.

FOLLOWING PAGE: *At the ports of call and in the different stopovers in a regatta, in addition to resting, stores and cooking materials also have to be stocked up, as is the case with this set of butane gas cylinders for cooking.*

The twin Club Med 1 *and 2 ships are also large luxury sailing ships, but in this case when it came to their design the hotel aspect predominated over their use as sailing ships. Their sails are totally computer-controlled and they are handled by a small crew. With their 613 feet draught, they can accommodate up to 400 passengers and 200 crew members, the majority of whom are hotel and catering staff.*

The Race brought together half a dozen maxi-catamarans which set out to sail round the world without any assistance or stopoffs for taking on supplies. One of the participants was the Polish Warta Polpharma, *which we can see in this photo just moments before setting sail in front of the Barcelona Olympic Port.*

In The Race, also called the Regatta of the Millennium, the two Club Meds, *the* Innovation Explorer, *the* Team Adventure, *the* Warta Polpharma, *the* Team Legato *and the* Play Station *took part. The winner was the* Club Med, *which sailed round the world in 62 hours, 6 minutes and 56 seconds, travelling 27,407.9 miles at an average speed of 18.3 knots. In the photo, the* Club Med.

almost 30-day voyage. Almost all the ships from the existing military and civilian sailing schools participated, as well as many belonging to private entities.

According to first-hand witnesses, at the time of the departure from Cádiz, when the numerous ships were taking up their sailing positions, it was totally unforgettable, since they were surrounded by a great throng of vessels of all sizes and types, including many ships from the Spanish navy, which co-organised the event.

PERIOD SHIP REGATTAS

Another type of regatta which is gaining currency of late, although large ships generally do not participate, is that known as period ship regattas. All the existing regattas of this type limit participation to historic ships – whose authenticity is recognised – or to period-style ships, i.e., those constructed recently using traditional materials and technologies.

Generally speaking, these are not fully-fledged regattas, since only runs between islands or continental shores and nearby islands are held, because it does not seem very appropriate to expose such valuable ships to the hazards of long-distance voyages, although at sea one never knows for certain where danger lies.

One of the most well-known and regular ones in Spain is the Don Juan de Borbón Regatta, or the Almirante Conde de Barcelona (Admiral Count of Barcelona), which was established in honour of the Count of Barcelona and is usually held during August in Palma de Majorca.

❏

CHAPTER IV

*A great sailing school, the
Juan Sebastián de Elcano*

A close view of the Juan Sebastián de Elcano, *which enables us to appreciate the presence of a topman – those who handle the yards are called topmen – standing on the foot ropes, tight ropes provided for the purpose underneath the yards.*

IV

There are not many large sailing ships – also called tall ships – currently at sea and in service: we specify "at sea and in service" since one does not necessarily imply the other. A tall ship can remain afloat moored to a dock, but that does not mean that she regularly sails. She can be visited as part of naval history, but there is quite a difference between that and setting sail, making several or quite a number of runs, although she may still be registered on a list, that is, she may officially be active.

One of the most illustrative cases of this is the *Constitution*, the U.S. Navy's *Old Ironsides*, a frigate built at the end of the eighteenth century, which is on the list of that navy's active vessels and thus has a crew and a corresponding budget or annual allocation, although she limits her outings to July 4th, and sometimes not even then. Another is the British *Victory*, a survivor of the Battle of Trafalgar, which also has a crew and budgetary allocation, although she is permanently berthed in one of the dry docks at the Portsmouth naval base, in the historical area.

The most common occurrence nowadays is for tall ships that regularly or periodically sail to belong to a navy or a company that operates them for cruises and pleasure voyages. Among the former are military and civilian sailing schools, and among the latter are sailing ships engaged in charter or scheduled trips. There is also another case: those belonging to foundations, NGOs or similar civic organisations. This situation, however, is readily comparable to either of the other two, since among this type of organisation there exist some whose yearly budgets are actually higher than those of certain so-called "third world" countries.

This is because the maintenance cost of one of these ships is so great that the idea of a single person having a fortune vast enough to be able to maintain one of these ships is now a thing of the past. One such case was the *Sea Cloud*, a four-mast barque built in Germany between 1930 and 1931, which was the personal yacht of the couple made up of the millionaires Marjorie Merriweather Post and Edward F. Hutton, and later a U.S. Navy ship (see the photos in Chapter 1), and today is engaged in luxury charter cruises.

In this respect, it is worth recounting an anecdote that is attributed to an illustrious Spaniard, a rich Catalan industrialist, the owner of one of the most beautiful two-mast schooners in the

PREVIOUS PAGE: *The* Juan Sebastián de Elcano *sailing with part of her sails aloft. It is worth noting that the light makes the sails appear transparent and allows us to see quite clearly the different tacks on the sails, especially on the fore topsails and the topgallant sail.*

The forecastle of the Juan Sebastián de Elcano *with her crew alert on port and starboard – preparing to enter or leave the port – with the manoeuvre clear and checking the spanker sail on the foremast.*

Juan Sebastián de Elcano's *mid-ships with people fastening the spanker sails to the spanker boom. Note that the stiff metallic rigging does not use lanyards – lines that run from deadeye to deadeye in order to tighten the shrouds – and that the use of inflatable or semi-rigid dinghies has almost completely replaced the traditional rowboat.*

Topmen or women – we cannot tell from the photo – on the Juan Sebastián de Elcano, *fastening the fore topsails. Note that the lower fore topsail furls onto the yard itself, while the upper fore topsail lowers the yard and sail. Two members of the crew are climbing along the ratlines of the shrouds to furl the topgallant sail (Photo: Albert).*

A topman climbing up the ratlines of the Juan Sebastián de Elcano *to reach his post. Note the belt or safety harness, which is required for climbing on the rigging to save falls.*

FOLLOWING PAGE: *Members of the crew of the* Juan Sebastián de Elcano *finishing fastening the mizzenmast spanker sail. Note the items used to control the ship's course: the helm wheel and binnacle, as well as the footropes hanging over the spanker boom.*

annals of history, the *Orion*, a fore-and-aft sailing ship with two spanker sails, gaff topsails, flying jibs and staysails, which was later sold to an Italian sailing school after being turned into the *Flying Dutchman* in the film *Pandora*. It is said that on one occasion, at the end of the 1940s, this illustrious person was chatting with two acquaintances who also owned and sponsored two similar ships of their own – the anecdote points out that these were the *Altair* and the *Rosalind* – when without any warning or formality, he was asked by an upstart about the possible cost of maintaining one of those noble ships, since "he was thinking of buying one". As the story goes, the answer he received was highly concise and suggestive: "If you ask me how much it might cost to maintain one of these ships, you don't have enough money to do so".

Unlike ships such as the *Sedov* or the *Kurzenshtern* – see also Chapters I and III – or the more modern *Pallada*, *Mir*, *Khersones*, *Tovaritch* and/or other similar ones belonging to civilian schools, all the tall ships or windjammers plying the seas today belong to navies; indeed, such is the case of the *Juan Sebastián de Elcano*, the *Amerigo Vespucci*, the *Cuauhtemoc*, the *Esmeralda*, the *Libertad*, the *Palinuro* and/or *Simón Bolivar*, among others, of which the *Juan Sebastián de Elcano* and the *Esmeralda* are considered to be

The *Juan Sebastián de Elcano, ready to set sail at the exit of the Port of Barcelona just after passing under the "Port of Europe" bridge. Note that the topsails of the two mainmasts are ready to be hoisted.*

One of the tops of the Elcano *with sails furled, in this case one staysail and one gaff topsail. Between this and the mast is a topman. On both ends of the top and through its horns, there is a backstay that also supports ratlines.*

The Juan Sebastián de Elcano *ready to set sail at the exit of the Port of Barcelona. Note that the mizzen gaff topsail is flapping in the wind ready to be hoisted, as are the square sails whose tacks are already wide open.*

A topman/woman aloft up one of the Elcano's *masts checking that all the rigging is clear and ready to be worked by the ropes on deck.*

The square sails of the Elcano's *foremast ready to be hoisted. From top to bottom, the topgallant sail, the upper fore topsail, the lower fore topsail and the foresail. Note the way sail is given to both fore topsails, hoisting the sail and yard of the upper fore topsail and hauling taut sheets on the lower fore topsail.*

A sequential series of photos of the Juan Sebastián de Elcano *hoisting her sails. On rounding the pier head, the mizzen and the fore main spanker sails start to be hoisted.*

The hoisting of these two sails continues, at the same time as the rest of the rig is being prepared to be hoisted in accordance with the standard procedure laid down for all types of wind conditions.

213

The two foresails, that is the fore main and the fore mast sails, are added to the two stern spanker sails, while the jib starts to be hoisted as well.

While the braces are manoeuvred so as to begin to guide the crossyards to the wind, the jib and the spankers continue to be hoisted. At the same time, some people are sent to the tops to prevent the possible snagging of a line.

The spankers and jib continue to be hoisted, as are the lower fore topsail and the inner jib.

Continuing with the hoisting of the spankers, the jib, the inner jib and the lower fore topsail, the yard and the upper fore topsail begin to be hoisted.

All the above-mentioned sails are still being hoisted while the topgallant sail starts to be unfurled.

With all the spanker sails and both fore topsails unfurled, the jib and inner jib are still being raised. The upper triangular sails, gaff topsails and staysails are not hoisted because of the wind.

With the spanker sails firmly set, the same is done with the inner jib, while the yards are braced in order to guide the two fore topsails.

The jib, which had been flapping until this point, is hoisted to the full.

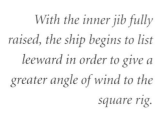

With the inner jib fully raised, the ship begins to list leeward in order to give a greater angle of wind to the square rig.

The fore topmast staysail begins to be hoisted and the foresail is unfurled. In the spanker sail on the foremast we can clearly see the reef-bands and the different tacks.

With the ship veering, the fore and topgallant sails are unfurled. The fore topmast staysail is still just beginning to be hoisted.

With its six triangular sails fully set, the task of unfurling the topgallant and foresail continues, as well as hoisting the fore topmast staysail.

The ship is still listing leeward to gain the angle of the wind needed to completely unfurl the topgallant and foresail. Even though no upper triangular sails – topsails and staysails – may be hoisted, crew members have been sent to the tops just in case these are needed.

With most of her sails hoisted, the Elcano begins to build up speed, probably reaching almost 10 knots.

With all her square rig hoisted, the ship sails at a good speed, although the fore topmast staysail is still not completely raised.

With its fore topmast staysail fully hoisted, the Juan Sebastián de Elcano *is sailing close to the wind. On this occasion, due to the wind conditions and the fact that this will be a short run, the upper triangular sails will not be raised.*

The Juan Sebastián de Elcano *sailing as seen from the starboard side. Note that the square rigging is very crossed, as it should be, and the spankers and especially the gaffs are wide open.*

In this photo of the Juan Sebastián de Elcano, *almost full on the stern, we can easily see the curving shape that the surface of the sails form when they are totally filled with wind.*

With tall ships the kind of tacking most frequently used is the so-called wearing. For this purpose, with the ship on course, the sheets of the spanker sails are hauled in to increase the hoist. Note that the fore mainmast spanker is hauled in very taut.

With the direct tailwind the spankers shift about, pushing the ship to the other side. Note that the fore mainmast spanker has already changed sides. Sailing with a tailwind and with the sails opened on either side is known as running before the wind.

Once the tacking is complete and all the sails have changed sides, the ship proceeds to sail on the new course.

The "spiral" effect on the surface of the sails is even more noticeable in this view of the Juan Sebastián de Elcano *from her portside.*

In this view of the foremast of the Elcano *the ropework of the sails and yards is quite visible. Gaff halyards, vangs, topping lifts, shroud levers, clew lines, buntlines, etc. can be seen perfectly.*

Climbing up the rigging on a large sailing ship is a job that does not frighten a well-trained crew, even less so today when safety harnesses are used instead of free climbing, as in the nineteenth century.

The moment of departure of the Great Cádiz-2000 Regatta. From left to right, surrounded by vessels of all kinds crammed with enthusiasts, the Gorch Fock, *the* Juan Sebastián de Elcano, *and the* Europa, *amongst other ships.*

PREVIOUS PAGE: *The running rigging of the* Elcano *is mixed, part metal and part made of hemp and synthetic fibres, as can be seen in this view of a block and tackle with two iron eyes, which has cables made of synthetic material and hemp ropes.*

The Juan Sebastián de Elcano *is lying to in order to pick up her dinghies. In this manoeuvre, part of the sails counterbalance the actions of the other part, so that the ship remains stationary in the water but ready to set sail by adjusting just a few lines (Photo: Albert Campanera).*

identical and among the most elegant, svelte, refined and lovely sailing ships ever to have sailed, while being controversial with regard to the naming of their rigging along with the *Libertad.*

The *Juan Sebastián de Elcano* was built by Echevarrieta y Larrinaga, the well-known shipyard in Cádiz, based on plans by the designers Camper and Nicholson from Southampton. At that time, she cost more than eight million pesetas. On 24th November, 1925, her keel was attached; she was launched on 5th March, 1927, and delivered on 17th August, 1928. Barring surprises, it is the oldest military sailing school ship in the world, since the *Amerigo Vespucci* was delivered three years later. The *Esmeralda*, her virtual twin and child due to the time difference separating them, was built in Cádiz as well, although due to the difficulties in Spain during the 1940s and 1950s that shipyard changed names – unwillingly – and years later went from being Echevarrieta y Larrinaga to Astilleros de Cádiz, S.A. The *Esmeralda*'s keel was attached on 30th May, 1946, she was launched on 12th May, 1953, and delivered to the Chilean navy on 15th June, 1954, since they had signed a contract to acquire her on 23rd October, 1952.

In fact, there was a third military sailing school ship in the same class as the *Elcano,* which was built according to the original plans, although slightly modified. This was the Argentinean *Libertad,* a country that in 1943 was interested in this type of ship, although with slightly different specifications, with the result that a modification was made in the actual rigging, going from having four masts to three, and from having brig-schooner to frigate rigging. All three ships have metal spars and masts, as well as fixed tackle.

As to the naming of the type of rigging on these ships, there are certain technical discrepancies in what some experts say on the matter, since they say that to be a brig a ship must have a three-piece foremast; i.e., it must have the lower, the topmast and the topgallant mast, and likewise with a frigate. At the very least, they claim it must be styled in the period of the wooden masts. But when metal masts, which are much stronger and more reliable, are used they are built in only two pieces, the lower and topmast. We should really call these sailing ships polacres then, such that it would be a polacre-schooner, in the cases of the *Juan Sebastián de Elcano* and the *Esmeralda*, and a polacre-frigate in the case of the *Libertad*. The *Palinura*, an Italian sailing school, does have the compulsory three-piece foremast, and is thus, according to the above-mentioned experts, inarguably a genuine three-mast brig-schooner.

The matter becomes even more complicated with respect to the names of the high square-rigging, since fore topsails are those whose yards use the topmast of the foremast for turning, or topsails on the mainmast, as well as topgallant sails when they do the same with the topmast. It could be that by accepting these theories, neither one of them would have topgallant sails – there are no topmasts, leaving only fore topsails and topsails, although there would be three or four of each, as the case may be. But, we are obviously getting far too complicated, and perhaps it is best to forget such purism and accept what the ship owners themselves, i.e., the navies of Spain, Chile and Argentina, believe. So we will consider the *Juan Sebastián de Elcano* and the *Esmeralda* to be four-mast brig-schooners, and the *Libertad* to be a frigate, without granting further consideration to the subtleties at stake.

As we can see in the photos, despite the fact that the *Juan Sebastián de Elcano* has already entered into her old age – after all, almost three-quarters of a century is quite impressive – we have to acknowledge that she wears her age quite gracefully, and continues to be a "lady" of the seas while also a swift "greyhound", thanks to her 20 sails, with a total of more than 32,291 square feet of canvas, something similar to the total area of five water polo pools.

The *Juan Sebastián de Elcano* replaced in her role as midshipmen's sailing school the frigate *Nautilus*, which in turn had replaced other ships before her. These gave their names to the *Elcano's* masts: *Nautilus*, *Asturias*, *Almansa* and *Blanca*, in memory of the previous sailing schools. The ship has made 75 training cruises, including various voyages around the world. She has been subject to different repairs and is expected to remain in active service until she reaches the age of 100.

One of *Elcano's* contemporaries until the end of the 1970s was the barque *Galatea*, formerly the *Glenlee* and the *Clarastella*, built in 1895, the marine sailing school bought by the navy in the "roaring twenties" whose end was not very flattering for Spain. Although different political groups had shown interest in it during the 1992 Seville Expo – claiming that they were willing to conserve her – she ended up being abandoned to chance on the shores of the Guadalquivir River, where she was taken to be broken. However, at the end of the 1990s she was bought by a British trust that has totally restored her.

❏

PERSONAL

- Albert Campanera
- Leo van Ginderen
- Javier Sánchez García
- Chris Sattler

CORPORATE

- Spanish Navy
- Port Authority of Barcelona
- Port of Barcelona Coastal Pilot Corporation
- Port of Cádiz Coastal Pilot Corporation
- Maritime Museum of Barcelona
- Organisations of regattas and meets:
    - Cádiz-2000
    - Cutty Sark 1996
    - Don Juan de Borbón
    - Cadaqués lateen sail meet
- Reedereij Clipper Stad Amsterdam
- Sasemar
- Star Clippers Corp
- The Race

Index